DATE	AUCTION HOUSE	ITEM WON	ITE LO			

DATE	AUCTION HOUSE	ITEM WON	ITEM LOST	PRICE PAID	ITEM VALUE	NOTES

DATE	AUCTION HOUSE	ITEM WON	ITEM LOST	PRICE PAID	ITEM VALUE	NOTES

DATE	AUCTION HOUSE	ITEM WON	ITEM LOST	PRICE PAID	ITEM VALUE	NOTES

DATE	AUCTION HOUSE	ITEM WON	ITEM LOST	PRICE PAID	ITEM VALUE	NOTES

DATE	AUCTION HOUSE	ITEM WON	ITEM LOST	PRICE PAID	ITEM VALUE	NOTES

DATE	AUCTION HOUSE	ITEM WON	ITEM LOST	PRICE PAID	ITEM VALUE	NOTES

DATE	AUCTION HOUSE	ITEM WON	ITEM LOST	PRICE PAID	ITEM VALUE	NOTES

DATE	AUCTION HOUSE	ITEM WON	ITEM LOST	PRICE PAID	ITEM VALUE	NOTES

DATE	AUCTION HOUSE	ITEM WON	ITEM LOST	PRICE PAID	ITEM VALUE	NOTES

DATE	AUCTION HOUSE	ITEM WON	ITEM LOST	PRICE PAID	ITEM VALUE	NOTES

DATE	AUCTION HOUSE	ITEM WON	ITEM LOST	PRICE PAID	ITEM VALUE	NOTES

DATE	AUCTION HOUSE	ITEM WON	ITEM LOST	PRICE PAID	ITEM VALUE	NOTES

DATE	AUCTION HOUSE	ITEM WON	ITEM LOST	PRICE PAID	ITEM VALUE	NOTES

DATE	AUCTION HOUSE	ITEM WON	ITEM LOST	PRICE PAID	ITEM VALUE	NOTES

DATE	AUCTION HOUSE	ITEM WON	ITEM LOST	PRICE PAID	ITEM VALUE	NOTES

DATE	AUCTION HOUSE	ITEM WON	ITEM LOST	PRICE PAID	ITEM VALUE	NOTES

DATE	AUCTION HOUSE	ITEM WON	ITEM LOST	PRICE PAID	ITEM VALUE	NOTES

DATE	AUCTION HOUSE	ITEM WON	ITEM LOST	PRICE PAID	ITEM VALUE	NOTES

DATE	AUCTION HOUSE	ITEM WON	ITEM LOST	PRICE PAID	ITEM VALUE	NOTES

DATE	AUCTION HOUSE	ITEM WON	ITEM LOST	PRICE PAID	ITEM VALUE	NOTES

DATE	AUCTION HOUSE	ITEM WON	ITEM LOST	PRICE PAID	ITEM VALUE	NOTES

DATE	AUCTION HOUSE	ITEM WON	ITEM LOST	PRICE PAID	ITEM VALUE	NOTES

DATE	AUCTION HOUSE	ITEM WON	ITEM LOST	PRICE PAID	ITEM VALUE	NOTES

DATE	AUCTION HOUSE	ITEM WON	ITEM LOST	PRICE PAID	ITEM VALUE	NOTES

DATE	AUCTION HOUSE	ITEM WON	ITEM LOST	PRICE PAID	ITEM VALUE	NOTES

DATE	AUCTION HOUSE	ITEM WON	ITEM LOST	PRICE PAID	ITEM VALUE	NOTES

DATE	AUCTION HOUSE	ITEM WON	ITEM LOST	PRICE PAID	ITEM VALUE	NOTES

DATE	AUCTION HOUSE	ITEM WON	ITEM LOST	PRICE PAID	ITEM VALUE	NOTES

DATE	AUCTION HOUSE	ITEM WON	ITEM LOST	PRICE PAID	ITEM VALUE	NOTES

DATE	AUCTION HOUSE	ITEM WON	ITEM LOST	PRICE PAID	ITEM VALUE	NOTES

DATE	AUCTION HOUSE	ITEM WON	ITEM LOST	PRICE PAID	ITEM VALUE	NOTES

DATE	AUCTION HOUSE	ITEM WON	ITEM LOST	PRICE PAID	ITEM VALUE	NOTES

DATE	AUCTION HOUSE	ITEM WON	ITEM LOST	PRICE PAID	ITEM VALUE	NOTES

DATE	AUCTION HOUSE	ITEM WON	ITEM LOST	PRICE PAID	ITEM VALUE	NOTES

DATE	AUCTION HOUSE	ITEM WON	ITEM LOST	PRICE PAID	ITEM VALUE	NOTES

DATE	AUCTION HOUSE	ITEM WON	ITEM LOST	PRICE PAID	ITEM VALUE	NOTES

DATE	AUCTION HOUSE	ITEM WON	ITEM LOST	PRICE PAID	ITEM VALUE	NOTES

DATE	AUCTION HOUSE	ITEM WON	ITEM LOST	PRICE PAID	ITEM VALUE	NOTES

DATE	AUCTION HOUSE	ITEM WON	ITEM LOST	PRICE PAID	ITEM VALUE	NOTES

DATE	AUCTION HOUSE	ITEM WON	ITEM LOST	PRICE PAID	ITEM VALUE	NOTES

DATE	AUCTION HOUSE	ITEM WON	ITEM LOST	PRICE PAID	ITEM VALUE	NOTES

DATE	AUCTION HOUSE	ITEM WON	ITEM LOST	PRICE PAID	ITEM VALUE	NOTES

DATE	AUCTION HOUSE	ITEM WON	ITEM LOST	PRICE PAID	ITEM VALUE	NOTES

DATE	AUCTION HOUSE	ITEM WON	ITEM LOST	PRICE PAID	ITEM VALUE	NOTES

DATE	AUCTION HOUSE	ITEM WON	ITEM LOST	PRICE PAID	ITEM VALUE	NOTES

DATE	AUCTION HOUSE	ITEM WON	ITEM LOST	PRICE PAID	ITEM VALUE	NOTES

DATE	AUCTION HOUSE	ITEM WON	ITEM LOST	PRICE PAID	ITEM VALUE	NOTES

DATE	AUCTION HOUSE	ITEM WON	ITEM LOST	PRICE PAID	ITEM VALUE	NOTES

DATE	AUCTION HOUSE	ITEM WON	ITEM LOST	PRICE PAID	ITEM VALUE	NOTES

DATE	AUCTION HOUSE	ITEM WON	ITEM LOST	PRICE PAID	ITEM VALUE	NOTES

DATE	AUCTION HOUSE	ITEM WON	ITEM LOST	PRICE PAID	ITEM VALUE	NOTES

DATE	AUCTION HOUSE	ITEM WON	ITEM LOST	PRICE PAID	ITEM VALUE	NOTES

DATE	AUCTION HOUSE	ITEM WON	ITEM LOST	PRICE PAID	ITEM VALUE	NOTES

DATE	AUCTION HOUSE	ITEM WON	ITEM LOST	PRICE PAID	ITEM VALUE	NOTES

DATE	AUCTION HOUSE	ITEM WON	ITEM LOST	PRICE PAID	ITEM VALUE	NOTES

DATE	AUCTION HOUSE	ITEM WON	ITEM LOST	PRICE PAID	ITEM VALUE	NOTES

DATE	AUCTION HOUSE	ITEM WON	ITEM LOST	PRICE PAID	ITEM VALUE	NOTES

DATE	AUCTION HOUSE	ITEM WON	ITEM LOST	PRICE PAID	ITEM VALUE	NOTES

DATE	AUCTION HOUSE	ITEM WON	ITEM LOST	PRICE PAID	ITEM VALUE	NOTES

DATE	AUCTION HOUSE	ITEM WON	ITEM LOST	PRICE PAID	ITEM VALUE	NOTES

DATE	AUCTION HOUSE	ITEM WON	ITEM LOST	PRICE PAID	ITEM VALUE	NOTES

DATE	AUCTION HOUSE	ITEM WON	ITEM LOST	PRICE PAID	ITEM VALUE	NOTES

DATE	AUCTION HOUSE	ITEM WON	ITEM LOST	PRICE PAID	ITEM VALUE	NOTES

DATE	AUCTION HOUSE	ITEM WON	ITEM LOST	PRICE PAID	ITEM VALUE	NOTES

DATE	AUCTION HOUSE	ITEM WON	ITEM LOST	PRICE PAID	ITEM VALUE	NOTES

DATE	AUCTION HOUSE	ITEM WON	ITEM LOST	PRICE PAID	ITEM VALUE	NOTES

DATE	AUCTION HOUSE	ITEM WON	ITEM LOST	PRICE PAID	ITEM VALUE	NOTES

DATE	AUCTION HOUSE	ITEM WON	ITEM LOST	PRICE PAID	ITEM VALUE	NOTES

DATE	AUCTION HOUSE	ITEM WON	ITEM LOST	PRICE PAID	ITEM VALUE	NOTES

DATE	AUCTION HOUSE	ITEM WON	ITEM LOST	PRICE PAID	ITEM VALUE	NOTES

DATE	AUCTION HOUSE	ITEM WON	ITEM LOST	PRICE PAID	ITEM VALUE	NOTES

DATE	AUCTION HOUSE	ITEM WON	ITEM LOST	PRICE PAID	ITEM VALUE	NOTES

DATE	AUCTION HOUSE	ITEM WON	ITEM LOST	PRICE PAID	ITEM VALUE	NOTES

DATE	AUCTION HOUSE	ITEM WON	ITEM LOST	PRICE PAID	ITEM VALUE	NOTES

DATE	AUCTION HOUSE	ITEM WON	ITEM LOST	PRICE PAID	ITEM VALUE	NOTES

DATE	AUCTION HOUSE	ITEM WON	ITEM LOST	PRICE PAID	ITEM VALUE	NOTES

DATE	AUCTION HOUSE	ITEM WON	ITEM LOST	PRICE PAID	ITEM VALUE	NOTES

DATE	AUCTION HOUSE	ITEM WON	ITEM LOST	PRICE PAID	ITEM VALUE	NOTES

DATE	AUCTION HOUSE	ITEM WON	ITEM LOST	PRICE PAID	ITEM VALUE	NOTES

DATE	AUCTION HOUSE	ITEM WON	ITEM LOST	PRICE PAID	ITEM VALUE	NOTES

DATE	AUCTION HOUSE	ITEM WON	ITEM LOST	PRICE PAID	ITEM VALUE	NOTES

DATE	AUCTION HOUSE	ITEM WON	ITEM LOST	PRICE PAID	ITEM VALUE	NOTES

DATE	AUCTION HOUSE	ITEM WON	ITEM LOST	PRICE PAID	ITEM VALUE	NOTES

DATE	AUCTION HOUSE	ITEM WON	ITEM LOST	PRICE PAID	ITEM VALUE	NOTES

DATE	AUCTION HOUSE	ITEM WON	ITEM LOST	PRICE PAID	ITEM VALUE	NOTES

DATE	AUCTION HOUSE	ITEM WON	ITEM LOST	PRICE PAID	ITEM VALUE	NOTES

DATE	AUCTION HOUSE	ITEM WON	ITEM LOST	PRICE PAID	ITEM VALUE	NOTES

DATE	AUCTION HOUSE	ITEM WON	ITEM LOST	PRICE PAID	ITEM VALUE	NOTES

DATE	AUCTION HOUSE	ITEM WON	ITEM LOST	PRICE PAID	ITEM VALUE	NOTES

DATE	AUCTION HOUSE	ITEM WON	ITEM LOST	PRICE PAID	ITEM VALUE	NOTES

DATE	AUCTION HOUSE	ITEM WON	ITEM LOST	PRICE PAID	ITEM VALUE	NOTES

DATE	AUCTION HOUSE	ITEM WON	ITEM LOST	PRICE PAID	ITEM VALUE	NOTES

DATE	AUCTION HOUSE	ITEM WON	ITEM LOST	PRICE PAID	ITEM VALUE	NOTES

DATE	AUCTION HOUSE	ITEM WON	ITEM LOST	PRICE PAID	ITEM VALUE	NOTES

DATE	AUCTION HOUSE	ITEM WON	ITEM LOST	PRICE PAID	ITEM VALUE	NOTES

DATE	AUCTION HOUSE	ITEM WON	ITEM LOST	PRICE PAID	ITEM VALUE	NOTES

DATE	AUCTION HOUSE	ITEM WON	ITEM LOST	PRICE PAID	ITEM VALUE	NOTES

DATE	AUCTION HOUSE	ITEM WON	ITEM LOST	PRICE PAID	ITEM VALUE	NOTES

DATE	AUCTION HOUSE	ITEM WON	ITEM LOST	PRICE PAID	ITEM VALUE	NOTES

DATE	AUCTION HOUSE	ITEM WON	ITEM LOST	PRICE PAID	ITEM VALUE	NOTES

DATE	AUCTION HOUSE	ITEM WON	ITEM LOST	PRICE PAID	ITEM VALUE	NOTES

DATE	AUCTION HOUSE	ITEM WON	ITEM LOST	PRICE PAID	ITEM VALUE	NOTES

DATE	AUCTION HOUSE	ITEM WON	ITEM LOST	PRICE PAID	ITEM VALUE	NOTES

DATE	AUCTION HOUSE	ITEM WON	ITEM LOST	PRICE PAID	ITEM VALUE	NOTES

DATE	AUCTION HOUSE	ITEM WON	ITEM LOST	PRICE PAID	ITEM VALUE	NOTES

DATE	AUCTION HOUSE	ITEM WON	ITEM LOST	PRICE PAID	ITEM VALUE	NOTES

DATE	AUCTION HOUSE	ITEM WON	ITEM LOST	PRICE PAID	ITEM VALUE	NOTES

DATE	AUCTION HOUSE	ITEM WON	ITEM LOST	PRICE PAID	ITEM VALUE	NOTES

DATE	AUCTION HOUSE	ITEM WON	ITEM LOST	PRICE PAID	ITEM VALUE	NOTES

DATE	AUCTION HOUSE	ITEM WON	ITEM LOST	PRICE PAID	ITEM VALUE	NOTES

DATE	AUCTION HOUSE	ITEM WON	ITEM LOST	PRICE PAID	ITEM VALUE	NOTES

DATE	AUCTION HOUSE	ITEM WON	ITEM LOST	PRICE PAID	ITEM VALUE	NOTES

DATE	AUCTION HOUSE	ITEM WON	ITEM LOST	PRICE PAID	ITEM VALUE	NOTES

DATE	AUCTION HOUSE	ITEM WON	ITEM LOST	PRICE PAID	ITEM VALUE	NOTES

DATE	AUCTION HOUSE	ITEM WON	ITEM LOST	PRICE PAID	ITEM VALUE	NOTES

DATE	AUCTION HOUSE	ITEM WON	ITEM LOST	PRICE PAID	ITEM VALUE	NOTES

DATE	AUCTION HOUSE	ITEM WON	ITEM LOST	PRICE PAID	ITEM VALUE	NOTES

DATE	AUCTION HOUSE	ITEM WON	ITEM LOST	PRICE PAID	ITEM VALUE	NOTES

Made in the USA
Columbia, SC
12 March 2022

57572051R00065